The Weight of Bodily Touches

The Weight of Bodily Touches

Poems by

Joseph Zaccardi

Joseph Zaccardi

-2019-

Cover design by Shay Culligan
Cover photography by Vidar Nordi-Mathisen

ISBN: 978-1-950462-28-5

Kelsay Books Inc.

kelsaybooks.com

502 S 1040 E, A119
American Fork, Utah 84003

In Memoriam

W. S. Merwin (1927-2019)

Animula vagula blandula
Hospes comesque corporis
Quae nunc abibis in loca
Pallidula rigida nudula
Nec ut soles dabis iocos

—*Hadrian*

Acknowledgments

Journals

Atlanta Review: "The Weight of Bodily Touches"
Baltimore Review: "Dupre"
ELJ: "To Hurt the Pain," "A Web" "Two Pairs of Windows" "Now Playing…"
California Quarterly: "Still Life at Sea" "Li Bai Returns to Jade Mountain"
Cincinnati Review: "Boy Leading a Horse"
Common Ground Poetry Review: "Girl with Mandolin"
Falling Star Magazine: "On a Winding Trail"
In Posse: "Civility"
Monterey Poetry Review: "This Is Where the Story Begins" "On a Cold Day in a Small Town Called Sunshine"
Nostos: "Behind the Trees the Music Rises" "The Making of a Poem by Confucius" "The Flute Song of Du Fu"
One: "To Feast on the Flesh of Decay"
Off the Coast: "Written on a Terrace Overlooking Two Enclosures"
Plainsongs: "The Body in Contour"
Poet Lore: "Talk in the Town Barbershop"
Potomac Review: "The Blind" "In the Valley of Windows"
Sonora Review: "What's Wrong with That Boy"
Spillway: "Picking Up After Others" "Watching the Waterwheel"
Stoneboat: "The Sound the Tree Makes"
Third Wednesday: "The Guitarist" "Journey from Point Pleasant" "Autumn and Her Auburn Hair"

Anthologies

Marin Poetry Center Anthology: "Watercolor" "Conversation at a Garden Party Under a Princess Tree" "Seed Clusters"
Poetic Matrix Press; So Many Voices: "Celestial Stems, Earthly Branches" "Black Sand River"
Sixteen Rivers Press; America, We Call Your Name: "The Ones Without Names"

Contents

Section Five

Section One

There are two ways to be fooled. One is to believe what isn't true;
the other is to refuse to believe what is true.

—Soren Kierkegaard

To Feast on the Flesh of Decay

Suppose first light spikes between limbs of the black ash
into the dog kennel where hounds brace their paws
against chain links and their spittle turns to vapor
as the farmer brings them water and a kettle of scraps
then goes back to the main house to help his wife in labor
and suppose he genuflects and counts her rapid breaths
and feels the thrum of blood move through her body
his trousers' knees and shirt sleeves wet as he waits
to catch the stillborn they've named Maia of the Angels
while outside a breeze rattles the wheat stalks and stirs
the chaff left on the field hayed days before it flowered
suppose this farmer returns to the barn for a shovel
to bury their child and in the rafters hears the rustle
of rats in the loft while his hounds bay to stalk a fox
while his wife Marta wraps their baby in white cloth
if you think everything disappears fully think again
suppose come late spring she digs up her child's
scaffold of white bones and presses them to her breast
to suckle her loss and what if she eats the grave dust
under her own nails and what if the farmer does
what needs doing back in the hayloft
by pushing down a bale of fodder
for the milk cows.

Girl with Mandolin

Elaine touches the scar where the surgeon cut through her sternum runs her finger over the raised red artistry that divided her body the way Picasso unbridled paintings to graft an art closer to life and she explained how the medical team pried open her chest how they used her radial arteries to make a bypass and how the stitches on her arms left trace lines from elbow to wrist that are smooth nearly opaque and she tells me about the store clerk who asked if she tried to kill herself who did not know the ancients pecked into patina of stone and chiseled with antlers their message why did he say such a thing she asks me and am I upset that a scalpel could craft such brilliance and then she struck the fretted fingerboard of her mandolin bringing the fullness of its sound to me from its hollow wooden cage and we who were separate are brought together our rooms and walls taken away.

The Body in Contour

You sit and hush the hurt of your new bruises
Pick up the newspaper left in the doctor's waiting room
Pull up your sleeves to show him the scars on your arms
Think about the story you read about how we came out of caves

You pick up the newspaper somebody left in the waiting room
It says read me and I will tell you everything you need to know
Says we came out of caves our bodies covered in matted fur
The words in today's paper claim they had no other choice

It says read me and I will tell you everything you need to know
It says trumpet vines always climb towards the light
The words in the paper claim they had no other choice
But to accept the whips of wind and rain and hail

It says trumpet vines always climb towards the light
Looking to where the sun settles in the west like a thief
They accept the whips of wind and rain and hail
The way scars fade yet leave an ache inside the body

Looking to where the sun settles in the west like a thief
Looking for a place in the woods only the lost can find
Your scars fade and leave an ache inside your body
Leave bruises and wounds ringing down in drops

And you remembered the story about how we came out of caves
How you pulled back your sleeves to show the scars you wore
After you picked up the newspaper left in the waiting room
And sat and hushed the hurt of your new bruises.

Without and Within

The day when something went missing
You gave me a cutout picture of yourself
And told me it's from a room without windows
And about the painting of two angels on the wall

You gave me a picture of yourself cut out
I cannot leave you nor your agony of existence
Nor the painting hanging on the wall of two angels
Back to back looking in different directions

I cannot leave your agony of existence you faced alone
When you took your shadow outside for a walk
Looking in different directions turning side to side
As you tried to fill holes and blanks with other blanks

When you took a walk outside in shadows where
You wore a mask with sutured lips and shuttered eyes
And tried to fill the blanks and holes with other blanks
I drew a picture of you so I'd know where you were

Wearing a mask with sutured lips and shuttered eyes
I replaced your picture you cut out of yourself
With the picture I drew of you so I'd remember
The day when something went missing.

A Web

Light cannot pass through this latticework without a trace set to waylay the unwary and because spiders are stoic and cagey they don't count days by days and they claim to always tell the truth as they weave lies to catch the foolhardy and wide-eyed off guard in undertones of locked-up barns and sheds and cellars secreted between joists and beams between crawl spaces and cripple walls and tonight which could be any night anywhere in a detached garage an old gas guzzler idles while its timing belt ticks and its steering wheel vibrates under a dirty skylight before a backdrop of shelved paint cans and a rack of hand tools and stacks of old newspapers in this space where a woman riding shotgun breathes tailpipe fumes anticipating a tripwire attached to a trap's latch slapping shut in a flash while the car's fuel gauge takes aim at empty and the green amp light glows on the dash as she sits cross-legged strapped into the bucket seat listening to earworms of radio static as she dream-shifts into drive to where high beams run ahead on a rural road to swallow road kill and broken white-lined blacktop.

Conversation at a Garden Party Under a Princess Tree

I said,
remember the creekside with logs
lined up like lounges, long wonderful
divans, mossy, leafy with dappled
yellowed bay leaves we crushed
between our fingers.
We talked about needing
each other.
You said
you could barely recall the creek,
nor the blue-diamond needles' soft
back and forth whisper,
our lips, nor what we said
to each other. You did remember,
though, the lichen-covered branches
and the way the sun would blind us
between their sway above our heads—
wasn't it eucalyptus, you said,
and weren't the dead logs
wet, infested with earwigs.
I said I never
remembered leaving.
You said you soaked
in a hot bath
scented with lilac
when we got home.
I too remembered that
and didn't know
what else to say.

Autumn and Her Auburn Hair

—San Francisco 2017

I glance at you on the #8 Market your right hand on the bus-strap your other hand holding a transfer as we trundle past the defunct Fillmore West where rock and scat and blues bled together back in '71 and in the end none of us will own our names not Aretha the Queen of Soul the falcon soprano not Brother Ray who hovered above his piano bench playing the blues of nowhere not the flower children lock armed in the crush of festival seating in this moment to moment concert played over and over in grooves that now belong to wind and time while the years diminish and days lengthen as we catch the #47 trolley going north onto Van Ness and turn our backs to our againstness in our separateness to stare eye-level at ad panels through stops and starts to Fisherman's Wharf where the bus's air brakes come to rest in their own breath where wails and yawps of seagulls echo in free fall and bay waters buss and hush the waterfront toward sleep and we're trapped in cycles tied in knots swaying side-to-side in a pod of people each body moving to their own beats in their own cages as I read a fragment from an ancient text posted above the back exit folding doors about a crane who lived for a millennium and how there was no one there to witness its beginning and end.

Boy Leading a Horse

The coffin's black lacquer the last prayer the needle in his vein and measure of smack aka white horse the mourners who howled who eulogized to change truth and why it is a waste of language such a waste of language for such thoughts in symbols and words and the enigma of why he butchered at the A&P supermarket why he hung quartered beef sides on hooks in reefers to bleed out the vital fluids rendered into fertilizer and blood meal why he carved meat off the bone beautifully his smile opening as he held a razor-sharp knife steady over the meat's grain the flesh unfolding on the heartwood cutting block why after each shift he used a steel scraper to rake away fat and meat then stiff-brushed and scrubbed the breakdown board over and over why he honed the boning knives then feathered them on diamond coated steels on each side why each night he fired up the hard crude tar why he fed warm black liquid under his skin his brain misfiring against a background of chaos as one body takes and gives license to solemnize the white powder's bitter taste to lessen the stigma of tracks on bare arms the way bare stands of black oak stand in bareness after the plunging hoofs are gone.

The Guitarist

Malcolm asked for solitude and when everyone left him he wandered the streets high and asked for silence just after he turned deaf the music stopped playing in his head and he feared for his sanity though not asking for loneliness it came down upon his shoulders and he teared up and jabbered and some said they heard his sobs in the Embarcadero Plaza in the early morning hours on top of that he asked for eternal peace and was assured by his signing-palm reader there'd be plenty of time later then he saw shadows and mouthed questions to them while they strayed off into corners and hid under his bed where spiders slept in the sound hole of his old guitar with the expended needles used to poison himself he asked why spiders carry sacs of poison but do not poison themselves he went blind then died then everything from his life was disassembled while everyone who had swayed to his strums came to the wake to lay eyes on his body but he was a no-show there was only a guitar's broken neck and tuning pegs as well as the strings and frets the waist and bridge bone and the fingerboard.

Accuracy

I learned
in the last half hour that a friend's daughter
died in a head-on collision.
Something instantaneous,
something as simple as that.

ICU

Walking the halls I hear the weary pulse of patients on lifesaving contraptions trapped and girdled by babel and a gurney casting chirps down a corridor pushed by an orderly while IVs beep and keep time to soundless drips and air whistles from tap holes during the midnight shift to first light all kept in sync by the on-duty nurse who gleams in her Day-Glo uniform her face all routine and I'm making up puns on the spot as when I say to her *I see you* and clear my throat and wheeze while a defibrillator delivers doses of electric current to undo a flatliner and lights flash on phone lines from callers ringing up to talk through their pain levels of guilt and remorse and I'm cuffed like a prisoner in lockdown who wants a reduced sentence because the jailed air here cannot escape my lungs and a voice shouts inside my body to be released on my own recognizance though I refuse to pay any bail upfront but do sign an advance directive to appear before white-coated sawbones for a heart bypass or angioplasty and such as I follow the blue tiles to the blue elevator door and feel its gears throb under my soles as it comes to rest on the fifth floor and the doors screech open and boy what I wouldn't give for a shot of bourbonized plasma and what it means to be useful and alive and in possession of a donor card that someday a doctor-to-be will decide if any of my parts are reusable or retoolable or if I'm worth the trouble to resuscitate from a morphine haze as I breathe with the help of an antiquated iron lung while my arms flap and my feet kick.

The Sound the Tree Makes

The tree fell in the forest because of deep freeze the tree fell because it was another day because of gravity the tree fell soundless onto shoulder-high snow the tree fell because the wind swirled because of root rot termite buggery because its torso was girded by bark beetles because the phloem and xylem dried the tree fell because it was time for it to fall it fell and the sound echoed and birds rose from their roosts the sound was train-like crushing thunderous the tree fell in slow motion black and white silent the tree fell because a lumberjack yelled timber because it was first growth old diseased the tree resting on the ground was delimbed by chain saws was cut into logs by bucking the trunk from butt to crown was dragged on a skid trail from forest to flatbed truck strapped down and hauled to the mill the outer bark skinned denuded with grinding wheels the tree was sized under a circular saw's buzz was kiln dried planed trimmed smoothed graded and banded the tree gave out a great scream when it was felled that could be heard by other trees in the next county but in some counties could not be heard at all.

Flying Geese Silent Woods

Bo Ya heard crackling hardwood in his friend's hearth and he asked him if he might retrieve this fine wood of an old spruce to craft a lute and even though the staves would be singed the soundboard would be flawless and he would carve a rose into its belly and veneer the neck with ebony turning one thing into another and to know the tone he would compose a song about a woodsman who would not fell a sawtooth oak because it was fire-blighted and bowed and scarred and years afterwards Bo Ya met his friend the woodcutter at a roadhouse where they spoke of bleeding trees how the sounds of the lute are like flowing water and hunger and the cook in cookhouse called out to his daughter to butcher one of two caged geese of which one could sing and the other could not *Which goose shall I slaughter* she called back to her father *The one that cannot sing* he answered then after one season turned to another Bo Ya learned of the death of his friend whereupon he smashed his lute for there was no one left to understand his music nor to hear the sound hole's deep groan and groundswell.

Section Two

In the kingdom of the blind, the one-eyed man is king.

—Desiderius Erasmus

The Ones Without Names

saw grunts cut off Charlie's ear to confirm a kill
saw these lugholes stowed in gunny sacks saw some guys
in Tiger Force recon wear them as necklaces or medals
saw them take not one but both ears to boot up the count
heard COs savvy to this ruse divide that number by two
then order GIs to cut and scoop the anus out instead
saw piles of man holes dried to hardtack treasured as trophies
saw hootches and huts burned down as M16s played taps
saw grenades launched into batches of women and children
read in *Stars & Stripes* how hawks on the home front growled
and hooted and groused about honor about dying to try out
new toxic agents and bigger bombs saw snapshots of doves
cooing for peace booing against war and peaceniks marching
for a pullout and the brass in the Pentagon bottleneck
goose-stepping and crowing in headlines and subheads
about light at the end of their tunnel
about the prey in a gunsight.

The Blind

At a traffic light in the theatre district a castaway sits sideways on the sidewalk on the opposite side of the street I see two holes for eyes a mouth twisted I cross toward her when the light turns green her face wrapped in skin of shadow she's dressed in charity clothes from houses of the poor from houses of the rich from many houses her outstretched hand awaits me in the early morning hour when the sun is low when my shadow is very long every day she reaches out for spare change I drop a few coins and pocket lint try not to touch her try to avoid the vacant glance because her eyeless glance accuses because there's a hint of unease on both sides of this transaction the way two actors in a bad play know they're part of a bad play on this busy street in this busy city where I pay out coins into a hand as though I were feeding a parking meter shamefaced my shadow covers this woman near the gutter cluttered with scraps and street dirt who doesn't know who I am doesn't know my name.

There's a Small Tear on a Canvas and for the Longest While It's All I Can See

Tell me tell me what news from the sky today she says
as light bends and bends and currents sway on the banks
of the Eel and for a second her eyes seem green instead
of cloudy gray when I ask her about her way of seeing
what she paints blind she says it is from her early and late
memories of sight and adds no beauty can be truly blissful
unless it is doomed to fade but tell me what news from the sky
today and I tell her the sky looks the way a sky does when
nothing's going to happen and I ask her how she envisions
and composes her paintings and she says she uses her night
as a paintbrush for the day and I look at her milky eyes again
and say *green* for no reason and she says she cries alone
in her room at night to be out of sight and tells me
her granddaughter asked if she could cry real tears now
that was the hardest question she'd ever been asked she says
and she answered her by saying the sky heals with rain
she then looks at the sky and her eyes are a kind of green
like light passing through silver maple leaves after a sunshower
she says she can see the color red when she closes her eyes
to the sun and after the sun sets we settle down
like conspirators around dying embers.

A Blind Man Singing

I write a few lines almost every day
scatter apple seeds and nothing much happens
I read back issues of poetry journals and listen
to old music that asks the same old questions
about love and blue skies and dark roads
I use words as bait to catch what I don't want to catch
and use my fingers to fish an olive out of my martini
and kiss the last piece of bread on my plate
salty brown crust and bone-white on the inside
to pull over me like a sheet and an old brown blanket
I know I can write whatever I want but it's mostly poetry
that comes out in the open from the ink in my pen
sometimes I imagine things outside my window
that are not really there such as a nightjar in a canoe tree
and every path I travel shrinks to fit my memory box
these days something is always leaving on its own
maybe that's why I meet myself running away in dreams
so before I forget here's a few strands from a yarn
told to me by my Uncle Alec who said he went blind
in his 60s from beating off each day for a leap year
but you can't believe everything he said for instance
he told me he could see the color red when he closed
his eyes and knew a woman who wrung the necks
of chickens and boiled their blood down to pudding
then he spat in his hat and crossed his heart to ward off
any hex but I didn't tell him he missed his hat and that
I could see the hurt where the light dimmed on his face
afterwards he told me about the unbearable music
going through his head and before he sang a blues song
about what the moon sounds like he warned me
to neither chime in nor look at him while he was singing
and one time he gave me a knife he claimed was used

to scalp George Armstrong Custer and said the worst part about being blind was he couldn't see people's reactions and he said this with his clouded and restless eyes.

Why Sometimes I Falter

There is always an opposition
between two people who love each other.
Take for instance the man and woman
I'm watching on the dance floor,
their smiles seem to be pasted on,
their shoulders stiff, backs straight.
Who is leading whom, who pushes and pulls,
and what is the purpose of the twirl
and bend in this tango, this music, this fight;
where the knees flex almost impossibly
and her hair whips, and their hands release
and come together. Each step practiced,
not one weaker than the other but equal:
the weight by balance, the muscular strength
by leverage, the unexpected look in the eyes
purposeful. This dance, a kind of genuflection,
a bestowing of grace. They finish, take
their seats, and are served fine food
and fine wine, and for the rest of the evening
they are tender toward each other and their lips
tremble, yes tremble, and I leave my plate
unfinished, there being so much.

Patient Room 4D

They told me about the morphine drip
said it would slow her breathing until
and stopped at *until* they asked for my consent
everything about this day was about form
everything indelible like invisible ink
her blank eyes the emptiness I signed

I remember hiking up the back of Half Dome
to an elevation of eight thousand plus feet
to about the point where I was out of breath
not *not* breathing but the way a child cannot
speak after running away from something scary
and my mother saying to me slow down
take your time so I said to her on this other day
slow down and when I climbed the last few steps
up the rope ladder to the baldhead of the dome
I was disappointed with no perspective there
there was just air and it didn't seem like much
and then coming down to flat land
I looked back on the face of the mountain
the mountain breathing back on me

Dragging its shadow over lupine and rocks
on this day the day my mother was born
I sing to her because there's still a chasm
that needs to be filled because thought is time
and immortality is one soul in many
the first full moon falling
across the valley floor.

Finding His Letter

Lucky recalls nights spent cruising alleys
and having sex with nameless men under conifers
and black locusts in parks and getting scratched
in brambles and brush and the deadwood
next to deadheaded hydrangeas where he found
twelve grave markers chiseled with Chinese characters
he then used as backyard pavers now covered in mulch
under the apricot bearing tree so sweet and juice full

Sometimes when you find something you keep its secrets
by losing it again

And though not ready to take a walk to the edge
Lucky's thinking about it and for his burial wants
a tree as a headstone he wants a memorial
sans candles sans flowers sans lies about how good
a guy he was he does not want to look better dead
than alive so tell the mortician no makeup
and if the cemetery caretaker won't allow a tree
because it is too messy then bury his whole body at sea
and if that's not green or PC enough because he's HIV
he wants his casket poly-strapped on a fire truck
with sirens blaring toward the crematory.

To Endure What Will Not Look Us in the Eye

In the locker room shower after track two high school jocks grunt and slosh in suds that rill torsos and legs around butt cracks and groins streaming sweat and soil to swill around the hair-clogged drain and after the shutoff valve squeaks the dribbles drip and circle their feet with soap scum and jizm while I sit across in the crapper stall peeking through door cracks after my twelfth lap between English Lit and study hall to listen and learn to keep my trap shut but things like this get outed about like loose lips sink ships and some rough stuff happens with knuckles and buckles and worse with words and threats and who can take this kind of shit not me hiding behind silence and guilt because two guys made a suicide pact and took their own lives for having touched each other and that's about all any of us from the class of sixty-five knew about queer fear because that was our view in our time and why we turned our backs on one another.

Bring Us Together

—The AIDS Quilt: The Names Project

Most things are black and white except for shadows
The weight of clouds hangs over the names on quilts
The doing and undoing of threads and knots and braids
There's nothing to see here move along move along

The weight of clouds hangs over the names on quilts
Hung on a wall sagging like carcasses being drained
Move along there's nothing to see here move along
A mother crochets a crying towel to savor the taste of salt

Hung on a wall quilts sag like carcasses being drained
Move along there's nothing to see nothing to see
A mother crochets a crying towel to savor the taste of salt
The clearest messages are the easiest to misread

There's nothing to see here move along keep moving
Pull a thread from a seam and a story unfolds
The clearest messages are the easiest to misread
A quilt reminds us what bolts of cloth can do best

Pull a thread from a seam and a story unfolds
Children love to skip stones and play at being dead
A quilt reminds us what bolts of cloth can do best
There's nothing to see here there's nothing to see

Children love to jump rope and play at being dead
The doing and undoing of threads and knots and braids
Move along there's nothing here there's nothing here
Except for shadows most things are black and white.

Now Playing…

About four men found spooned side by side like fillets in a cast iron skillet in an after hours rendezvous alley where their body fluids circle away from open wounds and their weals bloom and we're told via voice-over about the stale urine odor wafting as car wheels spin on the heady sheen the almost patent leather patina on the sweaty asphalt in this film noir where these scenes force moviegoers to focus blur and refocus on the streetlight's find before dawn swallows everything in its folds along this tenement row where caged windows are shut tight and parlor lights snap off even as shut-ins and busybodies strain to eavesdrop over the squawk box static of the rap of cops swapping fag jokes as the blink of the black & white cruisers' turrets click and clack even as one patrolman spreads a blanket over the vics as though this act of kindness mattered and at the end of the flick the soulless soundless movie credits slow scroll down screen to give stock-still audiences time to digest the coughing-blood language about love and loving being not enough.

The Burying Ground

I follow a fire road to a dead end spot in a forgotten wood where a statue of a freed slave stands before back-dropped clumps and stretches of spruce and fir trees whose tips appear like an arrow's fletching and though the plaque on the statue's plinth was pried off this man's right arm is raised his left hand hooked around chains his face knotted his bearing muscular and walking back the way I came my thoughts turn towards humans locked in cages towards where slavers on platforms auctioned off leg-ironed men and women and sold naked children who could not speak and who when they cried bidders and rabble alike wanted to know why they cried and how easy it is to forget the names of those made nameless by a twisted history and though penned words endure the weight weighs on unmarked graves covered by pavers set down for the living to walk upon.

Squirrel Cage

The inmates stroll and strut while turnkey Turner keeps eyes trained on the con nicknamed Sparks who handles two flowers in two paper cups of water round and round the promenade inside the circle of cubicles careful to not spill a drop who during lockdowns sits locked-up cross-legged on his rack and acts as though he's outside absent from himself and the miscreants and jailers caged in their own way do time shifts where day turns to night the night watchman signals lights out with three off/on/off incandescent flicks marooning the lighted globe strung up from a vaulted beam as the time clock turns round and round to midnight to when Sparks gulps his cups in swigs and balls the empties and shoots them through the ribs of his cell and cinches a white penny balloon of heroin to his arm and watches a cut flower fold its wings like lungs as night splits into mere seconds.

In the Company of the Mind

—The SHU: Special Housing Unit

I will speak of unquiet things and speak of quiet things *one two buckle my shoe* I will compose penless poems to leave and live outside in the middle of the night let me describe the darkening sky and a flower which can wither or bloom how grubs hibernate in dirt I will speak of honeybees that sting and die *shoo fly don't bother me* I will speak of a shaman's drums and rattles of their talking and prayer sticks and the flesh of sour apples and green water running off the pines I will dream of a green day dazzled in snow the conifers scarved in ice where lichen writes new stories on their dying bark *because I had no shoes* let me describe the shapes shadows make in the morning sun by sun and what happens when you look in a mirror and nothing looks back and describe jailbirds *who live in a shoe* and seek to deny their sentences their need to find something in the earthly ether of bodily want and how there is strangeness in a madman's eyes and quietness in a madhouse let me describe the pattern of a snake as it slips through grass and her young vipers on a cold spring day writhen and knotted together in a world created from suffering and depression the storm in the brain the tempest no one else can hear *if the shoe fits* let me describe the written word how it is stronger than the tongue and describe forgotten signs and marks on ancient pottery shards that ask is it not grievous to bury the dead with the living.

The Weight of Bodily Touches

—Thomas Hardy

Say window and windows open say gravity and all the stones return to their beds the things not said stay closed dead bolted doorjambed rip-rack of creek rock and cave-ins some days are like other days they walk around in seasons some day there will be a last day some call it redemption some call it fate in the beginning there were no days there were no nights some ask is the window half opened or half closed either way says the optimist lets the wind in either way says the pessimist lets the warmth out lets the cold in say ocean and vistas open say desert and sand dunes unfold *The Lady of the Lake* the man in the moon and some seas are said to be bottomless some celestial bodies light years away neither reachable nor graspable everyone carries the burdens of birth binding and bonding finding and untying every sage knows there's always a place in the woods only the lost can find and time surrounds them circles circle around time after a seven year drought in the M'Zab valley of the Saharan desert two or three children drowned trying to walk on water they had never seen before.

Solitude

Human beings inside cages figures of men behind crossed bars cons too strong to give up to give over to sleep in the long white-lighted nights making poems inside their skulls paperless poems by penless plotters who will cut someone for a cigarette for drugs for a Snickers bar and trade racist oaths trade lives who curse and spare no one who have turned bitter who kill time by slaying a bug who try to stem the flow of tears with tainted blood so time will torture them no more they've learned the lesson when you meet a wild beast the side who cries out first must beg for grace for they are sentenced not to years but to a life where wolves rule as lords and all others must pay in flesh and they call forth the La Fontaine fable about an old bone-weary woodcutter who sets down his load of firewood and groans and moans and calls out to Death and when Death appears asks him to help put the burden he owns alone back on his shoulder.

Silence of Falling Out of the World

I'm studying a touched-up and re-worked *bruin*-tinged painting that shows a squirrel mid-scratch on the bark of a dewy weeping willow whose ooze of pearls clings to its whip-like branches I'm tracking the brushstrokes of this artist who carved a relief of a woman on the backdrop of a stone wall with a palette knife and spread oil like tears brushing the moon in the fur of nightfall and feathered in the upper right corner an owl whose barred tail is tethered to shadow and in the bottom left corner brings to life a dark dog that conceals its fangs when suddenly a hawk's shriek strikes a note from outside my window and cuts through me this fall here in the season of orange and brown in the season when valley and black oak leaves genuflect and turn their warm colors away from the breeze as I mind-wander among the pines the castles of enchantment to feel the sap slowing and get caught up in a time-stream where the soul seems to come nearer to the bleed inside my body to the weary pulse of the inkwell that holds my words back to find what is flowing there where I recall the first time I was cut short in a moment of thought and saw a shrike impale its prey on thorns and how I was captured in the undertones of the understory of a world buried in debris in layers of years in decay where I stood in shade everything mangled and bruised.

Section Three

When the well is dry we'll know the worth of water.
—Benjamin Franklin

Dupre

Despite the wind and sting
I keep going back to a time
on the Golden Gate Bridge
when my school roommate jumped
on this side of sunset.
Witnesses saw him
remove his crucifix, bless
himself and go over.
I'd hate to have to tell you,
Dupre, that your family
came to the apartment and tried
to take my stereo. I gave them
your fine hand-painted plates
and the Lazy Boy you upholstered
in chambray. They looked disappointed,
but it was all you'd left.
I've missed you. And the black current
under the gate pulls me again
and again into its littered world.
The gulls and crabs
stripping, the softening
of whatever falls and rises.

Ernest Hemingway on a Bend in the Eel River

When she was out of the water I could see
her labored breathing, the way her body flexed and writhed,
and I say *she* was a *she* but what do I know about a trout's sex life,
only that the word *it* seemed wrong; her tail fin kicked up river
sand, and mica speckled her scales. I had to put my wet hands on
her then work my fingers into her gill to hoist my fourteen-inch
(make that eighteen inch catch), to peer
into the prism around her eyes,
                    then I bent my knees to ease
her back into the Eel and she seemed to take on the river's color
as she slippered off downstream; enchanted perhaps by my hand-
tied fly, she kite-tailed away from me. Back at camp
my fishing buddies sat on the ground smoking Havanas;
tackle and gear packed up, nothing to show for the day,
no passel of fish to brag over on the trek back to town.
I didn't tell them about my angling,
about the rainbow that chased my fly
out of the water,
and how she fell at my feet
and how I held her
and how she felt.

The Ocean Is Always on the Outside

Something today seems wrong—the Pacific is not pacific
and the sand along Kehoe beach is gray and dirty—I read
sometime after breakfast that the Japanese will resume hunting
whales and that their hearts weigh about two hundred
and fifty pounds—not the hearts of the Japanese the hearts
of whales—the ocean to my left means I'm marching north
one step in front of another over and over feeling pacific
the way the Pacific ought to as my mind runs sideways
in the poem I carry rolled up in my right palm where it holds
metaphoric tides and storms at bay like music in my head
and I close my eyes and it grows—not my head the poem
I compose—have you ever noticed how a fishing line seems
to bend obliquely at the point it enters water—this brings
to mind the parable of Han Hsin who went fishing in a river
and met a washerwoman who saw how hungry he looked
so she gave him food and he thanked her saying he'd repay
her kindness some day and she answered him angrily saying
she wanted no reward—I can feel this eclipse everything I lack
but I cannot bring back old bones and listen instead to the old
hocus pocus of waves pulling everything under its belly
then flatten as it tries to pacify with its shush and susurrus
and froth—I'm caught in the depth and breadth that waver
between existence and nonexistence between the dives
and clicks of whales—I'm overwhelmed watching
the shore's increase and decrease
the way words are not enough
and leave the wreckage
of no reward.

Addendum to this poem—

That no one can drown
in the Dead Sea
is a myth.

The Weight of Endlessness

I went outside barefoot without my glasses
onto the gravel path to the arbor covered
in full-leafed wisteria and sat like a stone
that does not change not tomorrow not in ten decades
and I carry one stone every day to my bed and before
I fall asleep I cradle my stone in my fist and when I wake
in the morning I can understand the talk of birds
and the ambient rumble of traffic as it crawls
across the valley floor

Living in fenced-in boxes between crisscrosses of roads
like a game of tic-tac-toe like chickens in cages
we teach the young by division for a reason for the right
way and the wrong way to spell a word and how to write
that word for the right and wrong reasons and that same
child's hand that learns to write learns to pick up
a stone and throw it

There's a saying in Chinese if you fall into a well
somebody will throw a stone in after you

Why do tyrants make a wasteland and call it peace
don't they know hatred never fails to destroy the hater
the blood that runs through us plays out day by day
like birds flying away in a mirror why look at abundance
and see desolation why stay all day inside and pretend to be
outside looking in and why carry the weight of a hammer
the curved shape of its handle fitted to the hand that wields
the maul that cracks rock into gravel to fulfill a need
that needs no doing for the end of the world
is always at hand.

Watercolor

—after Winslow Homer

I am so vast, to capture me in my white-on-blue light
he frames me with his hands, squares and measures
my unending moves. Without warning seagulls
cry aloud into watercolor, pleased to pose.
His brush floats out of sea, falls to his side.
I rest in his wash. He composes from
my transparencies a shape, a rise.
In a gallery of worlds gone flat, moving
before me hundreds of eyes.
Above clouds twisting.

Circle and Alchemy

For those who keep tally of things I'm grateful because between one week and another I confuse the days and the temperatures and I thank the man at the Guggenheim who said of Pollock's opus *There is not motion there there is the absence of stillness* and I can't remember if he was old or if it's just me doing memory-aging changing one thing into another the way yellow paint peels on a clapboard house and how it seems to slough from goldenrod to jonquil

And I thank too the poet who compared clouds to our souls on a canvas that contains itself within itself I always knew there were gods up there just never dawned on me it could be our spirits' likeness and I thank the spiders for their painstaking work because their art is both beautiful and hair-raising and I admire their dimensional designs and their single-mindedness in reweaving across the path I crisscross each day and how they un-puzzle the reason I wave wildly at what clings and trails behind me and how they rebuild because there is so much left.

Still Life at Sea

His mind is an incoming tide he never talks about where he lives no one knows his name it could be Jack-tar Sea-dog or Salt before dawn he fishes from shore with a long pole and hooks and cooks his catch in a sand pit over driftwood embers and sings old songs no one else remembers one after the other and always seems to be thinking always about to weigh anchor in his small schooner and never cares about the next landfall but looks instead at the sea as an unfinished canvas under sail and talks to himself and does not sing during this time for music is always with him he talks about the ocean gods their indifference to our existence how they are eager to punish the smallest nautical miscalculation and sees mortality as a color that trembles as the vain measurement of time sees the vast complicated clouds as a coast that cannot be reached and dawn as a rawness settling around a wound in a world grown smaller and thinks about his ketch how her fore-and-aft sails untangle the wind's embrace how she plows along the surface taking him to the edge to something painful and beautiful.

To Stray and To Scatter

Sand dollars
fly-encrusted seaweed
the dreck and detritus of sea break
blue snail shells
and a child's doll naked and sexless
eyes and make-up brined away
sun-blistered fake hair

There's a map in sand
known as coastline and wave break
this language problem solver
working over and over and over
with her throat music

There are
beached jellyfish pillows
a necklace tethered to sea grass
strung with the breath of foam
the calamus of a tern
a voodoo of needles

I scratch sand with a quill
this question
why is the carapace of a crab
though empty still beautiful
and hold my breath and wait
for feedback from water
from formless wind.

On a Cold Day in a Small Town Called Sunshine

On a cold day we traipse barefooted on the beach to feel the air to know what lies within and beyond the sea's edge where landfall meets land's end and you say a storm is coming and I say your name out loud to your shadow down there on the sand you leading you to places you have not been you say people who belong together need not be together after they partake of each other's shame together we find a bloated seal on dry sand whose eyes will not close we touch her gritty skin and nothing happens the laying on of hands brings both peace and pain in everything we do a part of us remains you talk of dying as something you could do by yourself and this same dark worm sleeps in both of us and I say I hate how breath rhymes with death where we find bare toe-to-heel imprints that end at high tide could it be someone plunged into the rip of the ocean or did someone backtrack to the small town's motel because there's nothing better than getting back together after breaking up and the tide recedes to uncloak ghost-like jellyfish and between a break in the clouds a wedge of cormorants flies on the wind's tail *We are looking in different directions* Thelonious Monk talking the talk of music said *you've been making the wrong mistakes* I say sunshine is a place in the throat of an hourglass a day gone and a day to come you laugh and say sound and time are seas to drown in when the shade we cast moves away.

Pull a Thread and a Story Unfolds

I was getting ready to meet Cindy
at the Hummingbird for brunch at our two-seater table
but when I get there she's stirring her teaspoon around
in her cup like a racecar taking sharp turns around a track
kicking up dust and grit and the way she shrugs her shoulders
and how her eyes dart from side to side betrays her mood
as a server brushes past me and says *did you want bacon*
with your Eggs Benny or a fruit cup she says *the latter*
and I say *I'll have the same as her* and cradle my mug
in both hands with my thumb resting in its lone ear
and blow dimples on the surface like a helicopter hovering
over brackish water but still burn my lower lip as I always do
but I didn't tell you yet about my friend who I've known
since the fourth grade when she taught me to jump rope
so I could outclass her girlfriends and in short order after this
my dad bought me a pair of boxing gloves and hammered up
a punching bag under our spidery cellar stairs as I smacked
at my face-of-the-day to hate rocking his head back and forth
asking for more though I never told my dad I loved those mitts
I also didn't let it be known that I couldn't hurt a spider or a tick
so what's wrong I say in about the way I'd ask a grease monkey
about a suspicious noise in a carburetor and she says *Rob*
(that's her dude boyfriend) *left her for her goddamned sister*
for God's sake she adds and starts to fan her face
with her menu and shoves the ripped open envelope at me
and I say *how retro to use the PO to send you a breakup letter*
that's got to take a month of Sundays in the dog days of August
then I almost say *behind every dark cloud is another dark cloud*
as is my habit when I want to commiserate the inevitable
but what comes out over my lower lip already starting to blister
is *I'll help you key that jerk's pickup truck* and for a second
the diner crowd and the waitress yelling *two Benedicts*

with fruit at the short order cook goes to dead air as on live radio
or at least that's the way it seems at the time and she smiles
and says *it's a deal* so even though every day starts about
the same on this day we drive out to the bay near San Quentin
to grab fistfuls of dirt along the bulkheaded shoreline and toss
them over the filthy incoming tide where a stiff breeze picks
it up and throws it back in our faces while a flock of terns
lets out screams like thieves that scored a windfall.

Two Pairs of Windows

—The Chinese character to paint 画 resembles a window 画

A dragonfly trapped between glass in a double hung
window trembles in the night for the night will not leave her
alone I study a painting of a homeless man who tries
to bite thru himself and I caress a bronze effigy of a drowned
woman tied in knots whose eyes will not close
in a kind of leaving and coming we use hand gestures
to greet and direct people and these same hands
can paint darkness in the night

I cannot not hold back nor block nor break these likenesses
to the living for who does not weep at night to be unseen
Blake wrote *There is a Moment in each day that Satan*
cannot find and I search for five minutes in the throat
of an hourglass for that moment and think about how
one more person in a room does not make a lantern
dimmer nor one person less make a lantern brighter
thru an open window I see an almost motionless biplane
hover on air currents its wings tipped toward earth
there's a sputter as the engine runs on into cloud cover
and then nothing

When I read words I see the blank paper behind the words
those windows to the outside and inside of things
for a window is an eye to the wind as daisies are
the eyes to a day and I see an abyss under every letter
as someone might scratch a scab over and over to reveal
a scar the membrane which holds the body together
if you write secrets on a window passersby will read them
in the brief time when warm air meets cool glass
for air is formless unless it inhabits a house

I listen to music when there's too much to bear
I listen to the lyrics of a singer's quiet singing
imitating silence I lift my pen from white paper
then let the stylus of my fountain pen touch
the blank page and draw a picture of a skylight
and listen for the rain to come
and listen for the rain.

There Is a Place Only the Lost Can Find

Near junipers
and overgrown yews I look down
at the breakers at Land's End to see my own self falling
into swells and I read the sign that says Danger
Area Closed as I listen to the sound-alike lyrics sung
by the sea singing over and over about life in the shallows
with the incoming tide hemming hawing and bussing
on hidden rocks and rusted rebar longing
for any passing crabber to embrace its graveyard

South of here
two windmills come to a standstill
while flocks of seagulls circle in search of handouts
I write this to record what I don't want anymore
the same way I stood before my class as a young student
and said nothing for fifteen minutes and received applause
equal to my measure about where we were going

Back in my 25th avenue flat
I watch a drowsy bluebottle on the windowsill
who seems to be watching me
finger a string of glass beads in my countdown
to the place where day and night part
to where I bury my sins the way
I'd bury a stray dog.

Section Four

The man who has a conscience suffers whilst acknowledging his sin. That is his punishment.

—Fyodor Dostoyevsky

What's Wrong with That Boy

Twelve years old has no friends and no use for his family has a paperback book jammed in his frayed jeans back pocket no it's a tin of Scripto lighter fluid has a burlap potato bag scavenged from an alleyway between shotgun flats has a barbed-wire cursive tattoo girding his left bicep and a cut on his lower lip dried to blood purple he's wrassled a stray calico by the scruff who claws and yowls as he stuffs her into that cat trap that he topknots tight then pisses on that writhing gunnysack no he squirts fluid from the tin then thumbs the striking wheel against the flint of his Zippo do you know what's on that brand around his upper arm attached to muscle hewn to bone do you know there is more to this.

Talk in the Town Barbershop

The talk is about war about history and how historians copy one another the talk is about a mind that is not there about absent friends the talk is about the abyss the red inner flesh of desire the dunes of another world the talk is about ailments and failures about the two-way stop sign in the town center installed after a child was run down by a red Impala the talk is about the Drakes Bay Oyster Farm in Tomales Bay being shut down by the National Park Service about the five-year drought and the recent rains softening the hillsides they repeat what they believe is true over and over as prayer how orphans beget orphans about a criminal's life and despair the talk is about sunflowers and the market price of copper the talk is about sighting a great blue heron at the watershed about the blue sky and the blue bay about how time flies just to keep up the talk is about black men being shot point-blank about sunrise obscured by a curtain of glaucoma the talk is about the whistle only dogs can hear and what humans spurn to hear.

The Amerasian

A mother will tell her son, when he comes of age, that his father
is an American who lives in a state where there is snow and sky-
scrapers. Until then, his questions about why he's different

she will leave to the wind, to the pastels of the forest.
She will give him a tin sword when he comes of age;
though it will rust it will give him the strength

to climb the areca and the date palms, to cut away the fruit.
When she tells him, he will brag to his friends that his father
will come to Vietnam to take him away. She tells him

every day to empty his bowl of noodles, finish his turnip cake,
his fried banana in syrup, so he will grow to be big and strong.
And as for her daughter, she will tell her the truth:

she will tell her she'll never marry, yet know many men,
and die young. Her daughter's questions she'll leave on the tides
of the ocean, on the heavy yellow heads of rice shoots.

Picking Up After Others

Uncle Henry who seemed to be from spring to fall
under the catalpa raking up fallen blossoms
then Indian bean pods then elephant-like leaves
and mumbling about what a mess this tree made
and saying my God when's the damn thing going to die
by which he meant he's tired of picking up after others
he wasn't really my uncle that was one of those stories
families make up for kids that lack any logic or genes
Henry's dead now but the old catalpa's still kicking debris
what makes this tree beautiful makes it also poisonous
I've learned to mistrust the gospel truth and trust instead
tall tales and the steadfastness of the worm who works
its way around to an apple's core then returns
to the red soil to the loam to the raw earth
that's me paging leaf by leaf thru an old Britannica
looking for evidence of the oldest living catalpa
and not finding anything about that space
between everything measured and listed
under *family trees.*

Belongings

The man on the corner holds his saxophone at his side
he does not sing about life on the streets or the scurry
of rats at night and of all things chants the lyrical line
I thought that my heartstrings were made of twine
then brings his sax to his lips and blows those notes
that crawl like snakes through traffic noise and smoke
while leggy strollers scoot by and avert their eyes
or glance at his upturned hat set out on the sidewalk
while a guy veers by arm in arm with a woman
and kisses her on the mouth and flips some change
that skitters and scatters over the bill of the sooty
Giants' baseball cap lying next to an old bluesy dog
who seems to sleep straddling forelegs and paws
around a black garbage sack bulging with belongings
they'll share as a pillow on this clear cold fall evening
outside the Orpheum after the last curtain call after
the cast takes in the bravos and the theater drapes fall
and the bandleader nods to his band in the shoebox
to stand as the man on the corner shoulders his axe
and harnesses his backpack to a scrap of cardboard
onto his back and chants and scats an old country line
that goes *should have read that detour sign*
and then picks up his spool of twine.

Under the Overpass

Homeless and nameless she bleeds from wounds no one sees she says the docs tried to put her out on the outside the cops in on the inside one hand is dirty-bandaged one sloe-eyed eye weeps she has a piston-rod heart ramming a crankshaft knows nothing about the shadows walking with her sometimes side by side sometimes in the lead or in empty spaces behind paths grown over with weeds and after each step she takes life turns up from underneath at first she remembers names then phrases that are stand alone thoughts then an image of an old graphite pencil drawing that shows a day at the beach a scene of swim-suited twins standing arms over each others shoulders and behind them swells the stilled ocean the exposure of silence lying with the horizoned sun in negative there's no leeward shelter no lifeguard or warning signs today she plies her scant belongings in a Safeway cart skewers a dumpster-found ballpark frank on a clothes hanger and warms it with a Clipper lighter under her tarped plywood home and she has a stray dog who shares her makeshift bedding it is said in cages the body shrinks and tigers forget how to roar between being and being between nothing and nothing in another scene she plays herself playing herself with another down-and-outer standing hand-in-hand singing and when asked what she wants mostly she says to die and live again and holds out her bandaged hand and makes a fist.

To Hurt the Pain

In the town square in the trees all is quiet the whispered shapes shadows make in the evening hour converge not the way light fades more the way darkness eclipses light how suffering holds us close the way a muscle spasm will not let go there are accidents without witnesses there are fatalities of unknown victims we are a handful of sand if we are anything the hourglass cuts the glass throat nearly in half someone has defaced the statue of an angel a homeless woman begins to weep she holds her knees to her chest rocks back and forth crushed by the weight of what hurts she talks in circles this is what the quiet accomplishes because it gives her nothing before her brain blooms like a perpetual rose when there is nothing left except being left alone or almost alone outside in the park's dim light where the white angel's shadow bows low before the white angel.

Journey from Point Pleasant

At the beach the lifeguard sits high on a throne
above swimmers and sunbathers his body trim
and muscular and shiny with coconut oil
his hair and eyebrows sun bleached and I think
I was seven years old when I saw him run
and dive into the ocean to pull a drowning man
from the surf and drag him limp and sea drizzled
ashore to put his lips over this man's mouth
lying prone in the sand and the lifeguard turning
this man's head to the side to expel foam
both of them giving and taking air in an embrace
and long after this day I thought why do we go
back to the sea to receive such treachery
but my family did return to our jetty-break beach
the next July my parents at rest under an umbrella
under a round yellow flower on this same Jersey sand
listening to the same rippling series of echoes
while I watched my brother run through the surf
running from something with his hands above his head
as though all of this was for him and everyone else
waiting to take turns there in the high noon light
that had shone on the breakers only last summer
for the man whose breath had gone to earth
never to return and for my brother who was found
a shade under twenty-five years later
drowned in a drug-induced depression
in a scuzzy Perth Amboy one-way alley
and all I can say now is *I had a brother*
and the last thing to see are the eyes.

In the Valley of Windows

In a gradation of gray seams in gray light
there's a crow perched on a power line crowing
I live half my time in thought in the other half try to solve
past mistakes it's not that easy the crow is saying listen
to the morning waken to the night crawlers' retreat
listen to a dog somewhere uphill who barks at shadows
(if you don't have a dog nearby do your own barking)
listen to a man and woman down in the downtown flats
he's saying he won't be home till late and she says
what's the difference when you're here you're not here
how awful it must be to be together and alone
by the time the barking dog has stopped barking
the day begins to emerge to revolve and resolve
the man slams shut his car door fires up the ignition
upshifts and peels out on loose gravel downshifts to a stop
for no answer is an answer for this is about not talking
it's about the curtain that falls between people
the day completes its arc the moon in the right part of the sky
the dog bedded down for the night dreams about squirrels
the crow waits and watches night's cover dissolve
and shadows return to their trees.

Bear Cave Mountain

Within the chamber's mouth Jeanette and Claude lie
on the cave's dusty bed the boy unlocks his zipper-fly
and digs under his pant waistband while the girl pulls up
her dress and feels the boy breathe hard feels him claw
over her to fit himself to her she raises one arm as his breath
moves from neck to lips angling his head this way and that
their skin smooth as felt in the warmth of night's suede
Jeanette sliding
                    Claude slipping as they hold on
before the opposing swaybacked ridge serrated and scarred
even as life will rearrange things over time while memories
edge towards the furred blend and bleed of a flashback
as seen through cloth to where their eyes will look
the way skies look when nothing's going to happen
they will try to find the map back to their cave and press
tracing paper to track their traveled course made over switch-
backs and shortcuts to uncover something valuable as a coin
with its gold face rubbed blank as the sun settled on that day
like a thief
like shade.

This Is Where the Story Begins

Alone the sun arises
to make the mountain laurel venomous
to make the mountain laurel vigorous

This is where the story begins

No life is unworthy of life
the days wound each other
a body worthy of being whole
comes apart
the difference
between truth and the end of words
one does not match lives to words
one does not match words to the world

This is where the story begins

Candles set before a vanity mirror
a miniature crèche and vials of essential oils
silhouette cutouts to chase evil spirits away
Tibetan prayer bells and singing bowls
and horses and reeds etched on red-lacquered urns
the ashes of lovers and lost stars
flesh and blood diamonds and dust
white bone chips

This is where the story begins

The dancer weaves her body
loosens her blackened hair
fastened with orangewood sticks
skin taut face drawn unseen

powdered bruises
her arms flail and float as she slides to the floor
a shapeless shape of silk and thread

This is where the story begins

Lucretius said the gods created the world
then vanished and left us to be alone to be all one
everything falls and everything resurrects
through a double-hung window the wind's dark eyelid
a collapsed shadow against a whitewashed wall
bells carry empty sounds across the barrens
a grain of sand evolves into a pearl
all things kill themselves

This is where the story begins

A search and rescue team
picks up the pieces puts them
in a body bag
so when his body hits the dirt
he is—says the medic—already dead
someone in platoon yells incoming
someone in the Quonset hut calls out
hit the rack
how many times do you turn
in your sleep asks the battalion shrink
the green lieutenant says I was asleep
so I can't really say but I know I've been
grinding my teeth
it's the sound in me coming out
I can neither turn it on nor turn it off
I just can't stand for anyone
to touch me

This is where the story begins

It's like being tied up and abandoned
a married man drops his pregnant girlfriend
the wife finds out and forgives him
a shaft passes through the body
the body falls apart
there are just too many pieces
to repair

This is where the story begins

The counselor asks the girl
if she has trouble sleeping
only when I'm awake she says
do you want the baby
I do and don't know
it's like being tied up inside
tie a knot a bow my tubes
and then palms up she holds out her arms
a sign of suicide
and surrender

This is where the story begins

The mountain surrounds and holds
yellow dust stretches down blue cliffs

This is where the story begins.

Section Five

When the winds of change blow, some people build walls,
and others build windmills.

—*Chinese Proverb*

On a Winding Trail

A long branch of willow has fallen
Across my path.

The sky is blue and empty.
There is always enough room on the ground.

An old dog greets me.
We both have easy temperaments.

When I was a boy I planted white birches
Above a wooden wall.

I worried they would not take root,
Worried there'd be no one to look after them after me.

My father told me when we're gone
The world would still exist,

I watched my father's eyes;
I did not believe him.

Li Bai Returns to Jade Mountain

I saw a tiger dozing in a hammock swagged between two ginkgos.
I saw a recluse sleeping on lichen and moss-covered stone.

I heard about a flock of geese that mistook rocks for an estuary
As dusk flared and faltered and distant peaks flamed.

I dreamed about a seabird searching for food and land;
I chanted a poem about a sailor and the glint on his battened sail.

I heard bells sound over a barren field and saw frost thicken
On a horse's mane before melting into a five-petal flower.

I walked on planed planks of a footbridge over a shoal of carp
While cicadas chirped in overhanging wild plums and willows.

I read stories about the ancient capital in the state of Chin
Where a rock was said to have advised its king.

I heard of a golden pheasant so enamored with his image
In a bronze mirror that he danced on and on until he died.

While I stopped to pick up fallen horse chestnuts, I saw a widow
Uproot brambles and weeds to plant yellow seeds of yarrow.

Watching the Waterwheel

A yellow boat approaches from downriver;
It is my neighbor come to drink my wine.
Maybe he wants to hear my poetry
And talk about flowers.

A few hours pass between us;
Willows shake away the day's dust.
Bees hover outside, then withdraw, then return;
Peach blossoms wait.

What can we give in return?
We share two bowls of wine.
He says an earthen bowl
Is as good as a jade bowl.

I tell my friend I have wine
Fermenting in the root cellar.
I tell him jade bowls are for fools,
Earthen bowls for friends.

The lees settle and we listen to the lyrics
Of birds below the timberline
To the flower-washing river.

Celestial Stems, Earthly Branches

If I could live in the woods among ferns and old pines,
I would fill a room with blue mountains.

In both places would be a fire and a flagon of wine,
And the days would breathe at either end and disappear.

What ceases to be is as natural as what comes to be:
Dried tea leaves release their fragrance to boiling water.

In sleep, the mind scatters briar and blackberry seeds.
Sows weeds and bean vines,
                                        sows reeds and tares.

Black Sand River

Peach petals drift downstream from a hidden world at peace;
Green birds feed among green rushes of the middle reaches.

Last year there was spring and this year spring;
Last year the mountain streams were still.

Last year the loquat blossoms shriveled.
Now the rains have returned.

In the woods the sound of trees falling.
Ten thousand trees surround one tree.

A brother and sister have drowned.
The nature of water is to be water.

Green birds in the floodplains;
Trees of jade and trees of pearl.

The rushes retreat and surge.
Who wants to be alone?

Behind the Trees the Music Rises

Near a hidden spring comes a song:
It is the oxherd boy playing the stone drums.

A girl labors over her loom,
Her blouse embroidered, her hair adorned.

She spins silk spools,
Works spindles and heddles,

Listens to the loom's treble and the drum's timbre.
She separates the warp threads

And makes a path for the shuttle.
She weaves a cloth as wide as her arm span.

On either shore of the Milky Way,
The vanishing river at daybreak,

Spinner and oxherd meet once a year,
Drifting-drifting-sky-earth-earth-sky.

Loom and drum,
Strand and stone.

The Making of a Poem by Confucius

A mother draws a chessboard on brown paper.
Her daughter fashions fishhooks out of old needles,

And a mouse patters along the skirting board,
And a spinner sits before her silk spools.

Last-chance peddlers cry out their wares;
The streams wind and the wind sings.

Crows and sparrows return to their nests,
Kestrels fasten onto their prey,

And dragon kites drift downward,
While white birds fade into the hills.

Waking in his bed half-filled with light,
Confucius said each poem starts as an iron bar

Hammered on an anvil into wire,
Then left to rest in a square inch of land.

The Flute Song of Du Fu

There are countless waves and still waters.
Older now, sleeping less and less,

Du Fu hears a messenger's call for those separated;
It comes from a wild goose snared in a river net.

This bird's pain is the same as his pain.
Its cries rise and fall and rise.

Wading knee-deep in water he frees this gosling,
Then holds her snuggling in his arms

And plucks from her wings three quills:
One for remembrance and two to feather his arrow.

What one gathers and scatters is windblown
The way red dust and willow tree fluff hover aloft,

The way he and she long for this day's release.

Greetings Lauren,

Let me start out by paraphrasing a story I read, some twenty years ago, about a conversation between Robert Lowell and Robert Frost: Lowell paid a visit to the venerable poet Frost at his home in Vermont, and in tears confessed he felt that all his poetry was bad, and Frost told him, "My dear, dear boy, don't you know we're all bad." I've struggled similarly with my poetry at times, and so I've sent you my latest book *The Weight of Bodily Touches* because it's hard for me to judge my own work. If you have the chance to read my book, and feel it's worth recommending to a friend or two, I'd appreciate that very much. Now I don't want to put you on the spot, so you don't need to tell me one way or the other your opinion of my poems or if you will recommend them to anyone or not.

Your friend in Poetry,
Joe

PS If you know someone who likes to write book reviews, please pass along my email joezaccardi@comcast.net and I'll send them a copy of my book.

PSS The book is available on amazon.com or
hppts://kelsaybooks.com/products/the-weight-of-bodily-touches

Seed Clusters

The sun is worn and dull over the southern river,
While white duckweed parts for a slow-moving scull.

A farmer raises the blinders on his dray horse, then rubs
down the nag's bay-colored coat with foxglove.

He thinks of ghosts still with him and ghosts gone away;
He hears the weave and beat and thrum of bees.

The harmony of sounds from times past scatters,
Then coalesces and gathers, then releases.

There are clouds flushed with radiant pearls;
There are early crickets that scrape and stop and crick.

What fills the ears idles mind and body,
And wind goes to wind and tears to tears.

Written on a Terrace Overlooking Two Enclosures

White clouds hover above South Mountain River
Like crystalline jewels on green treetop shrouds.

In a garden of knots, foul weeds and sweet herbs thrive,
And strings of blue algae billow on pond rocks.

I listen to katydids shrilling in the willows
And watch cook-smoke swirl above the village below.

Birth in morning, death by nightfall, the mayfly's fate;
The trace of 1000 years is no more than a worn path,

No more than a lifespan lies in its wake.
Streams cascade to filament within the well of the world.

Every day, poets unfurl, braid words out of their inkpots;
Their lyrics about the orioles makes no sense to orioles.

I listen to a boatman's oar-song creak, stroke, and touch.
There are ten thousand ways to a square inch of land.

Xuanyan-shi Writes About His Life While Watching Wild Rice Undulate

In my first year I thought of nothing; in my seventh year
My thoughts were of dragons and wars.

In my ninth year I scrawled characters on sand and rock,
Leaving them behind to wash away and grind down.

In the spring of another year I wore out the hours
Pining for beauty and greatness and blessedness.

In the summer of my middle years I chased animals
In clouds, let my horse gallop riderless and unbridled.

In the fall, turning older, I grew remorseful and morose,
And drank heavily and abandoned all common sense.

In the winter of my sixtieth year my hair turned white,
And I walked between graveyard poplars and stone drums.

I whistled my falcons back to my outstretched arm;
I looked upon the vast seas and great distances

And thought about the backwater's surge and sink,
About how a fisherman lost upon the great oceans

Thinks only of land and land's end.

About the Author

Joseph Zaccardi served as Marin County, CA poet laureate (2013-2015), and during his tenure published and edited *Changing Harm to Harmony: Bullies & Bystanders Project*. His poems have been published in *Cincinnati Review, Common Ground Review, Poet Lore, Spillway*, and elsewhere; his fourth collection of poems, *A Wolf Stands Alone in Water,* was published by *CW Books* 2015. He is a veteran of the American War in Vietnam (1967-1970).

Joseph says poetry came alive for him in the 6th grade when his teacher, Sister Francesca, gave him a small book of poems by W.C. Williams; a gift, alas, that he's lost. Perhaps the power of poetry is that it stays with you, even when it is not with you. He has no working process that he can recognize or describe. Each day is a tree of verbal apples one may climb; he is usually up there unless he is after the even more delectable fruits of silence. Each day he tosses seeds; each day he retrieves just sprouted words.

Notes

In the Memoriam to W.S. Merwin, I included the Hadrian poem, in the Latin, as a tribute to Merwin's translation of said poem; that translation is available online. The first book I read by Merwin, in 1996, was *The Rain in the Trees*, it so upset me because there was no punctuation that I went through the whole book and scratched in commas, periods, and semi-colons, etc. throughout. In 2003 I had a front-row seat to hear Merwin read at the Hearst Theatre in San Francisco. After his reading, I showed him what I'd done to his book, and said how wrong I was about all that. He laughed, turned away to get something out of his valise; it was an eraser, and then he signed his book for me. I still have the eraser he gave me.

The poem "To Feast on the Flesh of Decay" has its roots from the Islamic sacred books and from the Bible, e.g. in the Qur'an 49:12 it says "Does one of you like to eat the flesh of his dead brother?" and from Revelations 19:17 "…the angel standing in the sun calls all the birds of the earth to come to a feast. The birds will feast on the corpses of a variety of people…" and from Leviticus 26:29 "And ye shall eat the flesh of your sons, and the flesh of your daughters shall ye eat." Also, this poem pays homage to Robert Frost's "Home Burial" and to the literature of family grief.

The poem "Squirrel Cage" was inspired by my visit to the Pottawattamie County Jail in Iowa; supposedly named for the population of black squirrels in that area; it was a giant metal drum stacked with three floors of pie-slice-shaped cells, housed inside a building with steel-lined walls. There was only one door, and the jailer used a crank to spin the cells around to let prisoners in and out. It was considered a 19th-century marvel at the time of its construction but was shut down after two years of operation because the turntable gears kept jamming.

The title of "The Weight of Bodily Touches" comes from a line in Thomas Hardy's novel *Tess of the d'Urbervilles*. To wit: "She lay in a state of percipience without volition, and the rustle of the strays and the cutting of the ears by the others had the weight of bodily touches."

In "Belongings," the lines "I thought that my heartstrings were made of twine" and "should have read that detour sign" are from *Detour (There's A Muddy Road Ahead)* a Western swing ballad written by Paul Westmoreland in 1945. The use of the word "axe" is slang for a musical instrument and dates back to 1955. The instrument to which "axe" was first applied was for the saxophone.

In "Section Five," I've used some Chinese idioms and expressions, to wit: *Earthen bowls* are for the down to earth. *Jade bowls* are for the wealthy or pretentious.

The ox-herd boy and *the weaving maiden* refer to the Chinese legend of the stars Altair and Vega. The Milky Way separates these lovers, and they are allowed to meet only once a year on the seventh day of the seventh lunar month.

The Stone Drums of Qín are ten granite boulders bearing the oldest known stone inscriptions in ancient Chinese.

A *square inch of land* is a Chinese idiom for *the heart.*

The *flute* brings back thoughts of home. A *wild goose* is a messenger for those separated from loved ones, friends, etc.

The Chinese expression, *ten thousand,* is used to mean the indefinite multitude.

Foxglove is an herb capable of making animals glow with health. *South Mountain* came to have a kind of mythic stature as the embodiment of elemental and timeless nature.

Xuanyan-shi is the courtesy name of Huang-di, the first emperor of China, he also is known as the Yellow Emperor.

Made in the
USA
Columbia, SC
77906220R00062